D0904254

My United States

New Mexico

MICHAEL BURGAN

Children's Press®
An Imprint of Scholastic Inc.

Content Consultant
James Wolfinger, PhD, Associate Dean and Professor
College of Education, DePaul University, Chicago, Illinois

Library of Congress Cataloging-in-Publication Data
Names: Burgan, Michael, author.
Title: New Mexico / by Michael Burgan.
Description: New York, NY : Children's Press, an imprint of Scholastic Inc., 2018. | Includes bibliographical
   references and index.
Identifiers: LCCN 2017051021 | ISBN 9780531235669 (library binding) | ISBN 9780531250853 (pbk.)
Subjects: LCSH: New Mexico—Juvenile literature.
Classification: LCC F796.3 .B872 2018 | DDC 978.9—dc23
LC record available at https://lccn.loc.gov/2017051021

All rights reserved. Published in 2019 by Children's Press, an imprint of Scholastic Inc.
Printed in North Mankato, MN, USA 113

SCHOLASTIC, CHILDREN'S PRESS, A TRUE BOOK™, and associated logos are trademarks and/or registered trademarks of Scholastic Inc.

Scholastic Inc., 557 Broadway, New York, NY 10012

1 2 3 4 5 6 7 8 9 10 R 28 27 26 25 24 23 22 21 20 19

Front cover: Rock formations at Bisti Badlands
Back cover: Albuquerque International Balloon Fiesta

Welcome to New Mexico

Find the Truth!

Everything you are about to read is true *except* for one of the sentences on this page.

Which one is **TRUE**?

T or F   New Mexico is home to 30 different Native American tribes.

T or F   The U.S. government tests some of its missiles near Alamogordo.

Find the answers in this book.

Key Facts

Capital: Santa Fe

Estimated population as of 2017: 2,088,070

Nickname: Land of Enchantment

Biggest cities: Albuquerque, Las Cruces, Rio Rancho

UNITED STATES

New Mexico

Contents

Turquoise

What Represents New Mexico?

Cumbres & Toltec
Scenic Railroad

4

Albuquerque International Balloon Fiesta

3 History

How did New Mexico become
the state it is today? 25

4 Culture

What do the people of New Mexico
do for work and fun? 35

New Mexico chile peppers

This Is New Mexico!

Aztec Ruins National Monument

UTAH

San Juan

FARMINGTON

COLORADO

Rocky Mountains

OKLA

1 Chaco Culture National Historical Park

GALLUP

Petroglyph National Monument

2 TAOS

Sangre de Cristo Mountains

SANTA FE

3 Palace of the Governors

LAS VEGAS

Canadian

ALBUQUERQUE

University of New Mexico

National Hispanic Cultural Center

Rio Grande

NEW MEXICO

ARIZONA

TEXAS

Gila National Forest

White Sands National Monument

Pecos

ROSWELL

Western Heritage Museum

Gila

Carlsbad Caverns National Park

LAS CRUCES

4

TEXAS

MEXICO

N W E S

0 40 Miles

① Chaco Culture National Historical Park

This site has ruins left by Native Americans who lived in the region starting about 1,200 years ago. The largest building there had more than 600 rooms.

② Taos Pueblo

Native Americans have lived at Taos **Pueblo** for more than 1,000 years. The buildings still do not have electricity.

③ Palace of the Governors

Spanish settlers built this as a government building in 1610. The oldest continuously occupied public building in the United States, it is now part of New Mexico's state history museum.

④ Carlsbad Caverns National Park

At this national park, more than 100 underground caves have been discovered so far. There are still many more to find! The largest cave open to the public is 30 miles (48 kilometers) long.

TEXAS

The "sand" at White Sands National Monument is made of a mineral called gypsum.

CHAPTER 1

Land and Wildlife

Located in the Southwest, New Mexico is a sprawling state filled with deserts and other natural wonders. Only four states are larger than New Mexico. While big parts of it are flat and brown, New Mexico has many forests in its mountain areas. It is a state that lies high above many other parts of the country. Overall, the average **elevation** in New Mexico is almost 5,000 feet (1,524 meters) above sea level.

Plains, Mountains, and Deserts

New Mexico's land areas include a flat, grassy region in the east that is part of the Great Plains. The Rocky Mountains run south from Colorado into north-central New Mexico. West of them is the Colorado **Plateau**. The Rio Grande is New Mexico's longest river. In the north, it crosses through parts of the Rockies as it makes its way toward the Texas border.

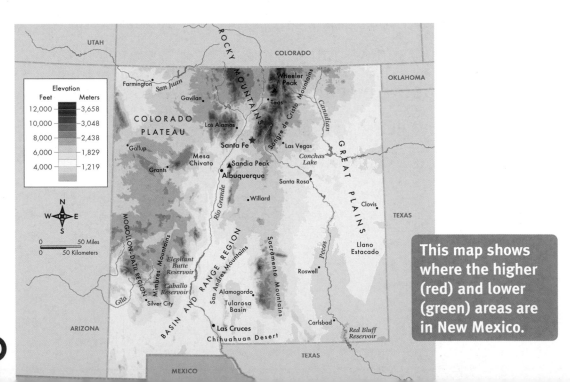

This map shows where the higher (red) and lower (green) areas are in New Mexico.

The Badlands of New Mexico

The Colorado Plateau is an area located in the northwestern corner of New Mexico. It is home to what are called badlands. Few plants grow there, and the region has many rocks that have been shaped over time by water and wind. The badlands also have areas where lava from ancient volcanoes has hardened into rock. Scientists have found dinosaur bones in some of these rocks!

Many of New Mexico's most scenic areas lie in the badlands.

Mountains and other rock formations are a common sight in the Colorado Plateau and Rocky Mountain areas of New Mexico.

Most of southern New Mexico is part of a larger region called the Basin and Range. Here, broad and flat desert valleys, or basins, lie between small mountain ranges.

In between the Basin and Range area and the Colorado Plateau is the Mogollon-Datil region. It has many volcanoes that formed millions of years ago.

Climate

Much of New Mexico is dry and sunny most of the year. But the weather varies in different parts of the state. The tallest northern peaks receive up to 300 inches (762 centimeters) of snow each year, and winter temperatures often drop below freezing. In the hot southern part of the state, summer temperatures above 100 degrees Fahrenheit (38 degrees Celsius) are common.

Heavy rains called monsoons often occur during the summer. They can quickly create powerful floods.

New Mexico's warm, sunny climate makes it perfect for outdoor activities.

MAXIMUM TEMPERATURE
122°F

MINIMUM TEMPERATURE
-50°F

Plants

With its wide range of weather and landscapes, New Mexico is the perfect home for many different kinds of plants. Yucca and cacti survive in dry desert areas by storing water in their leaves. Wildflowers of all kinds line many of the state's roads. Common trees include the cottonwood, juniper, and piñon. At the highest elevations, aspens and fir trees fill the forests. Aspen leaves turn a brilliant yellow in autumn.

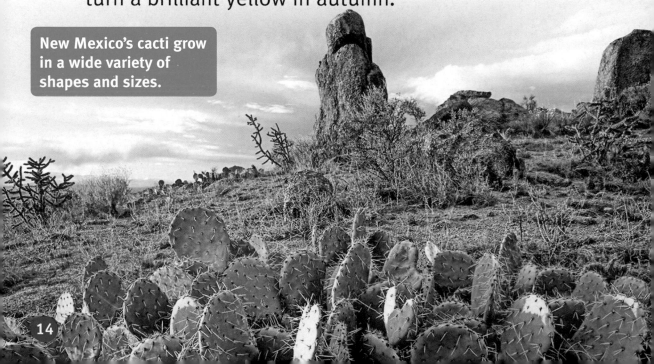

New Mexico's cacti grow in a wide variety of shapes and sizes.

The horns of a male bighorn sheep weigh more than all the bones in its body put together.

Animals

New Mexico has a great variety of animals, too. Elk and bighorn sheep are found in the mountains of the north. So are black bears and wild cats. Desert life includes many different reptiles, such as rattlesnakes and **endangered** Gila monsters. The state's birds include bald eagles, roadrunners, and many different kinds of hawks. The local rivers are home to fish such as trout and bass.

The New Mexico capitol has a collection of nearly 600 pieces of art, including *Tug O' War*, a sculpture by artist Glenna Goodacre.

CHAPTER 2

Government

New Mexico's capital city, Santa Fe, is the oldest state capital in the country. It was settled by the Spanish between 1607 and 1610 and has remained the center of New Mexico's government ever since. It is also the nation's highest capital city, with an elevation of about 7,000 feet (2,134 m). New Mexico's state capitol is called the Roundhouse. The building is the only round state capitol in the country.

Three Parts of Government

Just like the U.S. government, New Mexico's state government has three branches. The legislative branch is divided into the House of Representatives and the Senate. It makes laws for the state. The executive branch is headed by the governor and carries out the state's laws. The judicial branch is made up of courts that **interpret** the laws.

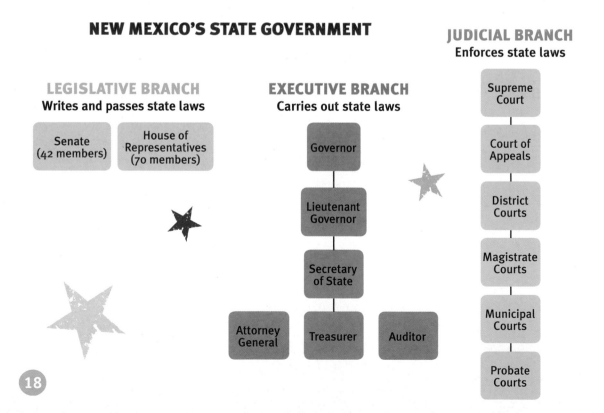

NEW MEXICO'S STATE GOVERNMENT

LEGISLATIVE BRANCH
Writes and passes state laws

- Senate (42 members)
- House of Representatives (70 members)

EXECUTIVE BRANCH
Carries out state laws

- Governor
- Lieutenant Governor
- Secretary of State
- Attorney General
- Treasurer
- Auditor

JUDICIAL BRANCH
Enforces state laws

- Supreme Court
- Court of Appeals
- District Courts
- Magistrate Courts
- Municipal Courts
- Probate Courts

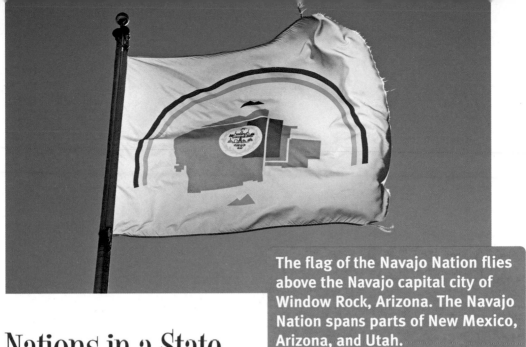

The flag of the Navajo Nation flies above the Navajo capital city of Window Rock, Arizona. The Navajo Nation spans parts of New Mexico, Arizona, and Utah.

Nations in a State

New Mexico has 23 Native American tribal nations, and each one has its own government. Members of each tribe elect their leaders. The 19 Pueblo tribes are led by governors, while the Navajo and two of the three Apache tribes each elect a tribal president. The Fort Sill Apache choose a tribal chairman. The tribes also have other elected officials as well as their own courts. The courts handle cases involving tribal members or nonmembers who live on or enter tribal lands.

New Mexico in the National Government

Each state elects officials to represent it in the U.S. Congress. Like every state, New Mexico has two senators. The U.S. House of Representatives relies on a state's population to determine its numbers. New Mexico has three representatives in the House.

Every four years, states vote on the next U.S. president. Each state is granted a number of electoral votes based on its number of members of Congress. With two senators and three representatives, New Mexico has five electoral votes.

2 senators and 3 representatives

5 electoral votes

With five electoral votes, New Mexico's voice in presidential elections is below average.

The People of New Mexico

Elected officials in New Mexico represent a population with a range of interests, lifestyles, and backgrounds.

Ethnicity (2016 estimates)

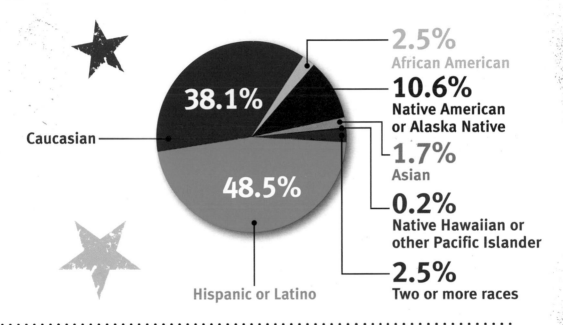

38.1%
Caucasian

48.5%
Hispanic or Latino

2.5%
African American

10.6%
Native American or Alaska Native

1.7%
Asian

0.2%
Native Hawaiian or other Pacific Islander

2.5%
Two or more races

10% of state residents were born in other countries.

77% live in cities.

26% of the population have a college degree.

84% of the population graduated from high school.

36% speak a language other than English at home.

68% own their own homes.

21

What Represents New Mexico?

States choose specific animals, plants, and objects to represent the values and characteristics of the land and its people. Find out why these symbols were chosen to represent New Mexico or discover surprising curiosities about them.

Seal

New Mexico's state seal shows a bald eagle standing behind a smaller Mexican eagle. This symbolizes New Mexico's transfer from Mexico to the United States. The Mexican eagle holds a cactus in one claw. In its mouth is a snake. This is a reference to an ancient Aztec legend. Beneath the eagles are the Latin words *Crescit Eundo*. This means "It grows as it goes."

Flag

New Mexico's flag features a symbol for the sun used by the Zia Pueblo people. The image is also called a Zia. The flag's red and yellow colors refer back to the flag of Spain, which once ruled New Mexico.

Red or Green (chile sauce)?

STATE QUESTION

Diners at New Mexican restaurants are often asked this question. If they want both red and green, they say "Christmas."

Biscochito

STATE COOKIE

These cookies are a popular treat during the Christmas holiday season.

Piñon Pine

STATE TREE

Many New Mexicans collect the seeds, or pine nuts, found in the piñon tree's pinecones.

Turquoise

STATE GEMSTONE

Many Native American artists make jewelry that features this gemstone.

Yucca

STATE FLOWER

This desert plant can reach a height of more than 15 feet (4.6 m).

Cumbres & Toltec Scenic Railroad

STATE TRAIN

This railroad runs high in the mountains of northern New Mexico between Chama and Antonito, Colorado.

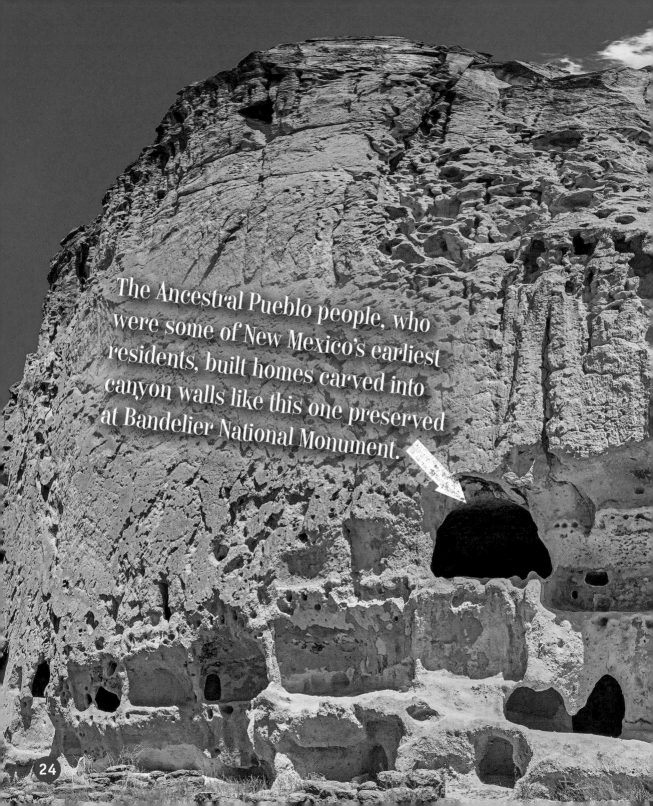

The Ancestral Pueblo people, who were some of New Mexico's earliest residents, built homes carved into canyon walls like this one preserved at Bandelier National Monument.

CHAPTER 3

History

For thousands of years, people from different parts of the world have called New Mexico home. They hunted, gathered, and later farmed in the dry desert climate. Over time, the large, open spaces and sunny weather brought people with new skills, and the area has blossomed into the state it is today. New Mexicans are proud of their history. They respect the past while always trying to make life better for the future.

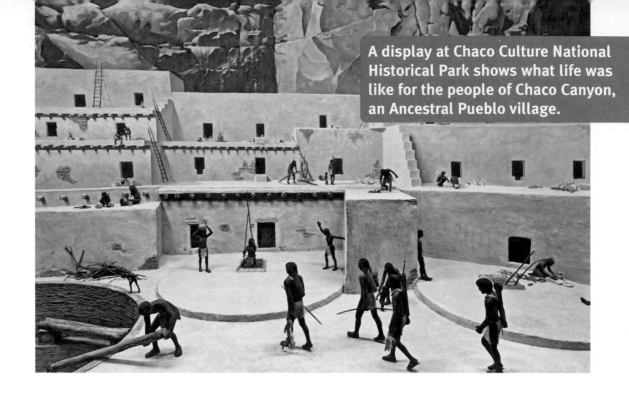

A display at Chaco Culture National Historical Park shows what life was like for the people of Chaco Canyon, an Ancestral Pueblo village.

The First New Mexicans

New Mexico's first residents came to the area about 12,000 years ago. They are called the Clovis, because items they left behind were found near the New Mexican town with that name. Over time, other cultures came to the region. These people included the Mogollon and Ancestral Pueblo. They grew corn, beans, and squash. They also hunted and gathered wild crops.

The Ancestral Pueblo were the **ancestors** of the Pueblo, who emerged in the area later. Like the Ancestral Pueblo, the Pueblo constructed large **adobe** buildings. Each building had many rooms. Pueblo men farmed and hunted, while women made pottery and baskets. The Pueblo were eventually joined in New Mexico by the Navajo and Apache peoples. By the 1500s, there was a wide range of thriving Native American settlements spread across present-day New Mexico.

This map shows some of the major tribes that lived in what is now New Mexico before Europeans came.

The Spanish Arrive

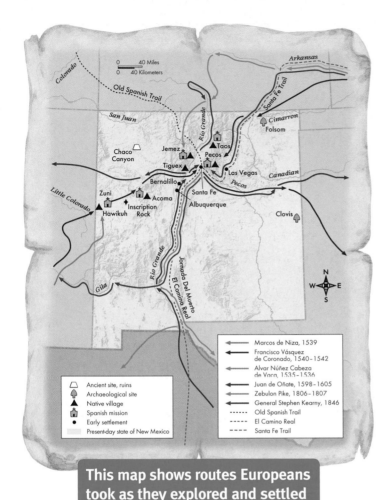

This map shows routes Europeans took as they explored and settled what is now New Mexico.

Map legend:

Symbols:
- Ancient site, ruins
- Archaeological site
- Native village
- Spanish mission
- Early settlement
- Present-day state of New Mexico

Routes:
- Marcos de Niza, 1539
- Francisco Vásquez de Coronado, 1540–1542
- Alvar Núñez Cabeza de Vaca, 1535–1536
- Juan de Oñate, 1598–1605
- Zebulon Pike, 1806–1807
- General Stephen Kearny, 1846
- Old Spanish Trail
- El Camino Real
- Santa Fe Trail

In 1540, Spanish soldiers living in the Spanish **colony** of Mexico headed north and explored present-day New Mexico. By the end of the century, they began to settle in the region, claiming it as part of Mexico. They wanted the Native Americans they met to give up their religions and become Roman Catholics. At times, the settlers tried to force the Native Americans to follow Spanish rule.

In 1680, members of several northern Pueblo groups united to fight the Spanish. This war was called the Pueblo Revolt. After it ended, the Spanish left the territory for 12 years. When they returned, New Mexico once again became part of the Mexico colony. Some Spanish New Mexicans began building new towns. They founded Albuquerque in 1706.

In 1821, Mexico won its independence from Spain. New Mexico became part of this new country.

The Pueblo Revolt of 1680 was led by a religious leader named Popé.

A U.S. Territory

In 1846, the United States went to war with Mexico and invaded New Mexico. It won the war, and New Mexico became a U.S. territory. This encouraged more American and European settlers to come to New Mexico. Some raised cattle on the Great Plains. Others mined for silver, copper, and other minerals. At times, the U.S. government battled Native Americans who refused to live on **reservations**.

Timeline of New Mexico Events

10,000 BCE
The Clovis and other early peoples come to New Mexico.

1706
Albuquerque is founded.

| 10,000 BCE | 850 CE | 1706 | 1846 |

850 CE
Ancestral Pueblo people begin building settlements in Chaco Canyon.

1846
U.S. troops invade New Mexico.

The American settlers did not always get along with the Hispanics, who had lived there for several hundred years. At times, the new settlers took the Hispanics' land. There was great mistrust between the two groups because of their differences in language and culture. For more than 60 years, this mistrust prevented New Mexico from winning statehood. Finally, it became a state in 1912.

1879
The first passenger train comes to New Mexico.

1945
The U.S. government tests the first atomic bomb near Alamogordo.

1850

1879

1912

1945

1850
New Mexico becomes a U.S. territory.

January 6, 1912
New Mexico becomes a state.

The first test explosion of a nuclear bomb took place in the desert near Alamogordo, on July 16, 1945.

Modern New Mexico

The discovery of oil and natural gas in the state helped create jobs for New Mexicans. So did the decision to base important military activities there. In 1943, scientists went to Los Alamos to build the atomic bomb. At that time, it was the most powerful weapon ever. The U.S. government tested the first bomb in 1945 and used two of them to help end World War II (1939–1945). Since then, New Mexican scientists have worked on many projects relating to weapons, energy, and climate.

Georgia O'Keeffe

Artists from around the world have come to New Mexico to work and live. One of the most famous was Georgia O'Keeffe (1887–1986). She visited the state often before buying a house in Abiquiu in 1940. O'Keeffe's paintings often show the scenery around her home. In 2014, one of her paintings sold for more than $44 million. It was the highest price ever paid for a piece of artwork created by a woman.

The Santa Fe Indian Market features the works of artists from more than 200 tribes. More than 100,000 people attend each year.

CHAPTER 4

Culture

The art of New Mexico dates back to the time of the Ancestral Pueblo and other ancient peoples. The pottery, weaving, and jewelry of today's tribes are prized by New Mexicans and visitors alike. Hispanic artists keep alive the art forms that Spanish settlers brought to the region. These include small wooden statues of religious figures, called *bultos*. Today, New Mexico is famous for both traditional arts and modern art of all kinds.

The Albuquerque Isotopes are a minor league baseball team associated with the Colorado Rockies major league team. This means the team's best players have a shot at moving up to the majors.

Sports and Recreation

New Mexicans don't just create art and visit museums. Favorite activities include hiking, hunting, and cycling. In winter, people can ski and snowboard on several mountains across the state.

New Mexico's baseball fans cheer for the Albuquerque Isotopes. This team plays baseball in a league just below the major leagues. Across the state, people love football and come out to watch high school and college teams. Soccer is also popular in many parts of New Mexico.

Festivals for Fun

Festivals called fiestas and feasts are held across New Mexico. They draw on the state's Spanish and Native American roots and often include religious celebrations. The Taos Pueblo harvest feast features men dressed as clowns. They compete to see who can climb to the top of a tall pole. One festival that attracts people from around the world is the Albuquerque International Balloon Fiesta. Hundreds of pilots come with their giant hot-air balloons.

The biggest event of the Albuquerque International Balloon Fiesta is the Mass Ascension, when hundreds of hot-air balloons launch into the sky at the same time.

Workers harvest chile peppers by hand on a New Mexico farm. New Mexico grows more of these spicy peppers than any state except for California.

Making a Living

Some New Mexicans work in factories or on farms. The state's farms grow crops such as hay, flowers, and nuts. They also raise cattle, sheep, and other livestock. Others help take care of the many tourists who visit the state. Movie and television companies film there because of its beautiful scenery. The state and national governments also employ tens of thousands of New Mexicans.

The National Labs

Scientists from all over the world come to work at the Sandia and Los Alamos National Laboratories. While the labs have a military role, the scientists also work on other projects. For example, at Sandia, in Albuquerque, some are working to create diesel engines that produce less pollution. Los Alamos scientists have tried to find new ways to increase the use of solar energy.

Scientists also come to New Mexico to work at the White Sands Missile Range near Alamogordo. The army develops and tests new weapons there.

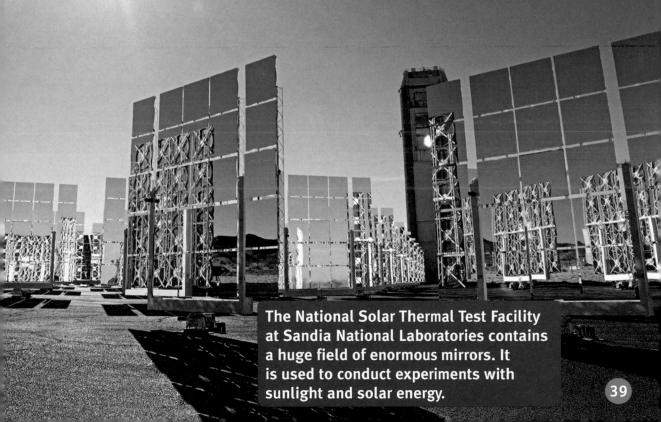

The National Solar Thermal Test Facility at Sandia National Laboratories contains a huge field of enormous mirrors. It is used to conduct experiments with sunlight and solar energy.

Spicy Delights

New Mexico farmers grow many crops, but the most famous are its green and red chiles. Some of the chiles are hot, while others are quite mild. In the fall, the smell of roasting green chiles fills the air. The roasted chiles are used to make sauces and stews. They also go on top of cheeseburgers and pizza.

 ## Green Chile Stew

Enjoy this spicy New Mexican dish at home!

Ask an adult to help you!

Ingredients

1 large onion, diced
2 cloves garlic, minced
2 tablespoons vegetable oil
7 roasted green chiles, diced
   (many stores sell them canned)
1 tomato, diced

2 tablespoons chopped fresh cilantro
$1/_2$ teaspoon cumin
$1/_2$ teaspoon coriander
$1 1/_2$ cups vegetable broth
Salt to taste

Directions

In a large pot, sauté the onion and garlic in the oil for 2 minutes. Add all the other ingredients, cover the pot, and bring to a boil. Then reduce the heat to simmer, remove the lid, and cook for 30 to 40 minutes. Enjoy!

Colorful murals are painted on the sides of many buildings in Santa Fe.

The Land of Enchantment

New Mexico's nickname, the Land of Enchantment, describes how many people feel about the state. Its natural beauty and rich culture make residents and visitors feel like they're under a magical spell. The state offers wide-open spaces and beautiful weather. New Mexico's past is still felt today, with the influence of Native American and Spanish cultures. New Mexico will always remain a great place to live, work, and play. ★

Famous People

Estevan Dorantes

(c. 1500–1539) was an African American former slave who helped lead early Spanish explorers into New Mexico.

Juan de Oñate

(c. 1550–1626) led the first group of European settlers into New Mexico in 1598. He treated the Pueblo people badly and was later brought to court for his actions.

Popé

(?–1692) was an Ohkay Owingeh Pueblo religious leader who helped organize the Pueblo Revolt of 1680.

Kit Carson

(1809–1868) was a trapper who also served as a scout for U.S. explorers and soldiers. His home in Taos is now a museum.

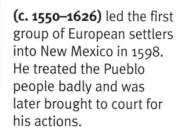

Billy the Kid

(c. 1859–1881) was the name given to a young outlaw who was also known as Henry McCarty and William Bonney. He took part in gunfights between rival groups in Lincoln County.

Maria Martinez

(1887–1980) was an artist from San Ildefonso Pueblo. She created a style of pottery that used black designs on top of a shiny black background.

Robert Goddard

(1882–1945) was a scientist who built the first rocket that used liquid fuel. He tested some of his later rockets in the desert near Roswell.

N. Scott Momaday

(1934–) is a Kiowa author and poet who has spent most of his life in New Mexico. His first novel, *House Made of Dawn*, won the Pulitzer Prize, and he often writes about Native American issues.

Nancy Lopez

(1957–) from Roswell, was one of the best women golfers in the world during the late 1970s and 1980s.

Susana Martinez

(1959–) became New Mexico's first female governor in 2011. She was also the first female Hispanic governor in the United States.

Did You Know That ...

Almost 30 huge satellite dishes outside Roswell pick up radio waves from space. Each dish is 82 feet (25 m) wide and weighs 235 tons.

During World War II, some Navajo New Mexicans became what were called Code Talkers. Their language served as a secret code that the enemy could not understand.

In 1898, during a war between the United States and Spain, future U.S. president Theodore Roosevelt led a group of soldiers called the Rough Riders. About 340 New Mexicans volunteered for this unit.

Some tourists like to drive on Route 66 through central New Mexico. This historic road opened in 1926 to link Chicago with Los Angeles. Parts of it were not paved for more than 10 years.

HISTORIC
NEW MEXICO
U.S.
66
ROUTE

On summer evenings, hundreds of thousands of bats fly out of Carlsbad Caverns. It can take up to three hours for all of them to leave as they begin to search for food.

Billionaire Richard Branson plans to send people into space from Spaceport America, outside the town of Truth or Consequences. They will pay $250,000 for a single flight.

Did you find the truth?

F New Mexico is home to 30 different Native American tribes.

T The U.S. government tests some of its missiles near Alamogordo.

Resources

Books

Bjorklund, Ruth. *New Mexico: The Land of Enchantment*. New York: Cavendish Square, 2016.

Hayes, Amy. *Native Peoples of the Southwest*. New York: Gareth Stevens Publishing, 2017.

Maine, Tyler. *New Mexico*. North Mankato, MN: Capstone Press, 2017.

Rozett, Louise (ed.). *Fast Facts About the 50 States: Plus Puerto Rico and Washington, D.C.* New York: Children's Press, 2010.

Taylor, Charlotte. *Get to Know Georgia O'Keeffe*. New York: Enslow Publishing, 2016.

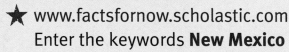

Visit this Scholastic website for more information on New Mexico:
★ www.factsfornow.scholastic.com
Enter the keywords **New Mexico**

Important Words

adobe (uh-DOH-bee) a building material made of clay mixed with straw and dried in the sun

ancestors (AN-ses-turz) people who lived long ago who were related to people alive today

colony (KAH-luh-nee) a territory that has been settled by people from another country and is controlled by that country

elevation (el-uh-VAY-shun) the height above sea level

endangered (en-DAYN-jurd) in danger of becoming extinct, usually due to human activity

interpret (in-TUR-prit) to figure out what something means

plateau (plah-TOH) an area of level ground that is higher than the surrounding area

pueblo (PWEH-bloh) a village consisting of stone and adobe buildings built next to and on top of one another; pueblos were built by Native American tribes in the southwestern United States

reservations (rez-ur-VAY-shuhnz) areas of land set aside by the government for a special purpose, particularly land that belongs to Native American groups

Index

Page numbers in **bold** indicate illustrations.

About the Author

Michael Burgan has written more than 250 books for children. He first visited New Mexico in 1996 and went there several more times before moving to the state in 2011. He lives in Santa Fe with his cat, Callie.